A Little Canadian Cookbook

Faustina Gilbey

ILLUSTRATED BY KAREN BAILEY

Appletree Press

First published in 1994 by
The Appletree Press Ltd
19–21 Alfred Street
Belfast BT2 8DL
Tel. +44 232 243074 Fax +44 232 246756
Copyright © 1994 The Appletree Press Ltd.
Printed in the E.C. All rights reserved.

A Little Canadian Cookbook

A catalogue record for this book is available in
The British Library.

ISBN 0-86281-468-5

9 8 7 6 5 4 3 2 1

Introduction

Welcome to Canada!

For over three centuries pioneers, adventurers, explorers and traders from around the world have been tempted to Canadian shores, often with nothing more than "ten dollars and a dream". They were our early Canadian forefathers and, as they settled across Canada, they packed with them the cultures, customs and cooking of their homelands. In these recipes Canadian cuisine is represented as originating from the first of these settlers, the French and English, and the original native peoples.

In contrast to those former days, the modern Canadian cook now has a magnificent choice of home-grown produce featuring wheat, wild rice, corn, maple syrup, salmon, beef, cheese, bacon, oysters, clams, squash, fiddleheads ... and much, much more!

To truly understand a place you must eat the local food. Canada, a mixture of old and new, has a cuisine both old and new. Enjoy and experience, therefore, the vastness and richness of Canada through a cuisine that has in it the rhythm of the people, the breath of northern winds, the whisper of prairie grasses, the majesty of high mountains and the tang of great oceans.

Note on measures

Metric, imperial and volume measurements have been given for each recipe. Recipes are for four, unless otherwise stated.

Lumberjack Camp Coffee

Coffee is always on the brew in Canada and the lumberjack camp is no exception. The original logger's breakfast of fried salt pork, bannock, blackstrap molasses and tea was eaten before dawn in silence under the strict gaze of the camp cook. Today's lumberjacks sit down to a man-size breakfast that starts and finishes with dark, strong coffee, "thick enough to eat."

Put 1–2 tablespoons of ground coffee per person into a pot. Fill up to the top with water and heat on the stove. Crush 2 or 3 eggshells, stir into the coffee and let it sit. The eggshells will collect all the fine granules and act as a strainer. Skim off any froth from the top, pour into mugs and drink.

Green Tomatoes, Peameal Bacon
and Fried Apples

Originating in Ontario, peameal bacon is salt- and sugar-cured unsmoked back bacon rolled in fine cornmeal. Combined with crisp green late fall tomatoes and glossy red McIntosh apples from the rich farmlands and orchards of Ontario, this seasonal breakfast makes a truly mouthwatering start to the day.

4 slices peameal bacon or	3 green tomatoes, thickly sliced
Canadian back bacon	2 tbsp butter
3 tbsp flour	3 red apples, cored and
pinch salt	thickly sliced
½ tsp black pepper	½ tsp cinnamon

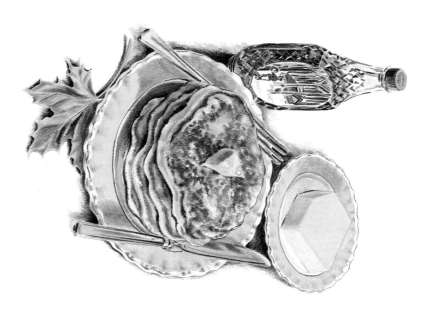

Heat a frying pan and fry the bacon. Remove, drain on paper towels, and keep warm. Combine the flour, salt and pepper and dredge the tomato slices in this mixture. Fry in the bacon fat until lightly browned on both sides. Remove from the pan and keep warm. Wipe out the pan and melt the butter. Add the apple slices and cook until lightly browned on both sides. Sprinkle with cinnamon and serve with green tomatoes and peameal bacon.

Stampede Buttermilk Flapjacks with Maple Syrup

Calgary is the cattle ranching centre of Canada. Its annual summer rodeo, the Calgary Stampede, attracts cowboys and cowgirls from all over North America. Chuckwagon breakfasts are a feature of any prairie public event. Flapjacks are flipped; eggs are fried "over easy," or "sunny side up"; platters are piled with sausages, bacon and hash browns and over it all is poured lashings of butter and maple syrup.

4oz/125g/1 cup flour	½ pt/12 fl oz/1¼ cups buttermilk
1 tsp baking powder	1 egg
pinch of salt	2 tbsp melted butter
(makes 4)	

Sift the flour, baking powder and salt together in a bowl. In a separate bowl, mix the buttermilk, egg and butter together and pour into the flour. Beat just until smooth. Grease a frying pan lightly and pour ¼ cup batter into the pan. Cook until lightly browned on the bottom and bubbly on top. Turn and cook the other side. Serve hot with butter and maple syrup.

Snow Muffins

Winters can be long and hard in parts of Canada, with temperatures down to 50° below and more. Not even skiers, snowshoers and hockey players want to be outside. From Moose Jaw, Saskatchewan, comes a recipe for which you need only open your door an inch, scoop out fresh, crisp, clean, snow from the porch and scurry back to your toasty warm kitchen with its smells of home baking. When Voltaire described Canada as "several acres of snow", he just didn't see the potential!

8oz/250g/2 cups flour	zest of ½ orange
3 tsp baking powder	3 tbsp melted butter
4oz/125g/½ cup brown sugar	4oz/125g/½ cup raisins
pinch salt	1½ cups dry snow or clean
scant ½ pt/8 fl oz/¾ cup milk	frost scraped from your freezer
½ cup orange juice	(or 2 eggs)

(makes 12)

Pre-heat the oven to gas mark 6, 400°F, 200°C. Sift the flour, baking powder, sugar and salt into a bowl. Stir in the milk, orange juice, orange zest and butter and mix well. Fold in the raisins and snow and pour into greased muffin tins. Bake for 15–20 minutes.

Pumpkin Apple Streusel Muffins

Modern-day pioneer Ann Henry came originally from Ireland to a horse ranch in Ontario, travelled by train to Banff in the Rockies, and then bicycled 800 miles to the West Coast where she opened her own café. Enriched with soured cream, pecans, apples and spices, Ann's fragrant muffins capture that robust earthiness and zest typical of Canadian home baking.

Topping:

4 oz/125g/½ cup finely chopped pecans
2oz/50g/¼ cup flour
3 tbsp sugar
2 tbsp softened butter
½ tsp cinnamon

Batter:

12oz/350g/1½ cups flour
4oz/125g/½ cup sugar
2 tsp baking powder
¼ tsp baking soda
1 tsp cinnamon
¼ tsp allspice
¼ tsp ground ginger
¼ tsp salt

Egg mixture:

2 eggs
⅔ cup cooked fresh pumpkin purée or tinned
2oz/50g/⅓ cup soured cream
2oz/50g/¼ cup melted butter
8oz/250g/1 cup cubed unpeeled tart apple

(makes 12)

Mix together topping ingredients in a bowl until the mixture resembles fine crumbs. Set aside. Sift together batter ingredients and stir well. Break eggs into a bowl and whisk in the pumpkin, soured cream and butter. Stir in the apple. Pour the egg mixture into the batter and lightly fold in. Spoon the mixture into greased muffin tins and sprinkle the topping over the muffins. Bake in a pre-heated gas mark 5, 375°F, 190°C oven for 20–25 minutes.

Sourdough Starter and Pioneer Bannock

Prospectors and adventurers of the 1800s heading to the Cariboo and Klondike goldfields carried their own "gold" with them in the form of sourdough starters. Cooking on open fires in the wilderness, doubling up their gold pan as a frying pan, prospectors made "home-cooked" bannock to help sustain their dreams of wealth.

Starter:

½ pt/8fl oz/1 cup milk
8 oz/250g/1 cup flour

Bannock:

10oz/300g/1¼ cups flour
pinch of salt
1 tbsp baking powder
3 tbsp oil
1 cup sourdough starter

For the starter, mix milk and flour together and leave in a warm place for 24 hours until sour and bubbly. Store, covered, in a glass jar or plastic container. When using, always leave 1 cup of starter and replace the rest by adding ½ pt/8 fl oz/1 cup milk, 8oz/250g/1 cup flour and 1 tbsp sugar, and leave for another 24 hours. You can keep this going for years and the longer you keep it and use it (about once a week), the better it gets. You can also freeze it, but leave it for 24 hours at room temperature before using.

For the bannock, mix all the ingredients together and knead gently. Pat out the dough to ½ in/1 cm thick and place on an ungreased baking sheet. Brush the top with milk and bake in a pre-heated gas mark 7, 425°F, 220°C oven for 20–25 minutes. You can also fry it, pioneer style, in a lightly greased cast iron frying pan until brown on both sides and hollow when tapped (about 10 minutes each side).

Habitant Pea Soup

Madame St. Denis of Val David in the Laurentian Mountains, just north of Montreal, remembers this recipe. Still a favourite Quebecois dish, this hearty soup would have warmed many a winter's night for the early French settlers. Serve this pea soup with corn bread and one of Canada's excellent cheeses, sharp Cheddar from Ontario, or creamy Oka, a type of Port Salut, from Quebec.

8oz/250g/1 cup yellow or green dried peas (or use split peas)
1 ham bone or ¼ lb/115g salt pork
2–2½ pts/1½ ltrs/4–5 cups water
2 onions, chopped
1 onion studded with 5–6 cloves
1 carrot, chopped
1 stalk celery, chopped
1 bay leaf
2–2½ pts/1½ ltrs/4–5 cups water
salt and pepper to taste
bacon bits
chopped celery leaves

Soak the peas overnight in cold water. Drain and put into a large saucepan. Add the remaining ingredients, except bacon bits and chopped celery leaves, and bring to the boil. Turn down the heat, cover and simmer over a low heat for 2–3 hours or until thick and creamy, stirring occasionally. Discard the ham bone or salt pork, pour the soup into warmed bowls and sprinkle with crisp bacon bits and chopped celery leaves.

Seafood Bouillabaisse

The essence of a good bouillabaisse (apart from spelling it correctly!) is the freshness of the fish. In earlier days fishermen's wives would be waiting on the shore with a roaring fire and a cauldron of steaming bouillon and vegetables ready for the freshly caught fish and clams, mussels, scallops and oysters to be thrown straight into the pot. Boiled furiously, it was served over mounds of thick bread or "hard-tack" biscuits.

2 tbsp olive oil
1 onion, chopped
2 tomatoes, chopped
3 cloves garlic, chopped
1 potato, diced
1 bay leaf
1 tbsp fennel seeds
1/2 lb/250g halibut steak, cubed
1/2 lb/250g cod fillet, cubed
2 pts/40 fl oz/4 cups fish stock

1/2 pt/300ml/1 cup white wine
1/2 lb/250g clams, washed
1/2 lb/250g mussels, washed
1/2 lb/250g raw prawns, shelled
1/2 tsp powdered saffron
salt and pepper
4 slices toasted French bread
2 garlic cloves, peeled
chopped parsley

In a large frying pan, heat the oil and sauté the onions, tomatoes, garlic, potatoes, bay leaf and fennel seeds until they start to brown. Add the halibut, cod, fish stock and wine and boil vigorously for about 10 minutes. Stir in the clams, mussels and prawns, season with saffron, salt and pepper, and cook for a further 5–8 minutes. Rub the toast with raw garlic cloves and put in the bottom of soup bowls. Pour the bouillabaisse over the bread and decorate with chopped parsley.

Fresh Oysters

After a day sailing through the warm waters of Desolation Sound north of Vancouver, drop the anchor and go oyster picking at low tide. Slurp them raw with neat vodka, or eat them piping hot straight from the barbecue with garlic breadcrumbs, lemon juice and hot sauce. Peaceful and glowing from the summer sun, watch a black bear patiently fish for his salmon supper at twilight.

16 oysters, shucked	freshly ground black pepper
2 drops vodka or rye whisky	Tabasco
lemon wedges	coarse salt or crushed ice

Arrange the oysters on their half shell on a bed of coarse salt or crushed ice. Add two drops of vodka or rye whisky to each oyster, add a squeeze of lemon juice, a sprinkle of black pepper and perhaps a drop of Tabasco (not for the purists) and eat quickly. Down they slide … fresh, glorious oysters plump with the taste of the ocean.

Maple Pork and Beans with Dill Beer Bread

The French Canadians call this dish *Fèves au Lard* but it was, and is, enjoyed throughout the country as Pork and Beans or Baked Beans. According to Madame Jehane Benoit, the patron saint of Canadian cuisine, the beans were cooked in a cooling outdoor brick oven right after the bread was baked. Bake your dill beer bread in the morning. When it's done, turn down the oven, and slowly simmer your beans, savouring every smell and listening to every succulent splutter as you anticipate the big meal.

Maple Pork and Beans

1lb/500g/2 cups white navy beans	4oz/125g/½ cup brown sugar
water	1 tsp mustard
2 onions, chopped	½ cup tomato ketchup
1 tsp salt	½ tsp oregano
½ lb/250g salt pork, left	½ tsp chilli powder
whole or sliced	salt and pepper
3 tbsp/¼ cup maple syrup	
or molasses	

Wash the beans, place in a large saucepan and cover with salted cold water. Soak overnight. Drain, cover with fresh water and bring to a boil. Simmer over medium heat, uncovered, for about 1 hour or until softened. Drain and reserve the liquid. Put the beans into a casserole dish and stir in the onion, salt pork, maple syrup, brown sugar, mustard, tomato ketchup, oregano, chilli powder, salt and pepper. Add the bean cooking liquid to cover, topping up with boiling water if necessary. Put the lid on and cook in a gas mark 1, 250°F, 120°C oven for 7–8 hours, adding more boiling water if necessary. Remove the lid for the final hour of cooking.

Dill Beer Bread

12oz/350g/1½ cups plain	½ tsp salt
white flour	1 tbsp dill seeds
8oz/250g/1 cup whole	½ pt/12 fl oz/3/4—1 cup beer
wheat flour	1 egg
1 tbsp sugar	3 tbsp oil or melted butter
1½ tbsp baking powder	1 tbsp milk

Sift the flours, sugar, baking powder and salt into a bowl and stir in the dill seeds. Beat the beer, egg and oil or butter together and

mix into the dry ingredients. Knead lightly on a floured board, form into a round, cut a slash in the top, brush with milk and bake in a pre-heated gas mark 4, 350°F, 180°C oven for 50–55 minutes.

Saltspring Island Lamb with Honey, Mustard and Rosemary

The Gulf Islands off the coast of British Columbia, with their gentle climate and smooth-barked arbutus trees, harbour wild plants, herbs, orchards, fish, game and the renowned lamb of Saltspring Island. Try to find some of the rare fireweed honey from the Peace River Valley in Northern British Columbia. Its pale clear colour gives it the name "white-water" honey.

1½–2½ lb/750g–1 kg	2 tbsp vinegar
rack of lamb	2 tbsp cider
2 tbsp honey	1 tsp rosemary
3 tbsp oil	salt and pepper
2 tbsp Dijon mustard	¼ pt/4 fl oz/½ cup dry cider
1 tbsp dry mustard	

Whisk the honey and oil together, then beat in the rest of the ingredients, except ¼pt/4 fl oz/½ cup cider, until thick and creamy. Rub the lamb all over with this mixture and bake in a gas mark 6, 400°F, 200°C oven for 20 minutes (rare) to 30 minutes (well done). Remove the lamb to a warm plate, add the ½ cup cider to the juices left in the pan and stir until bubbling. Strain and pour over the lamb.

Tourtière and Green Ketchup

Tourtière is a French Canadian speciality traditionally served on Christmas Eve following Midnight Mass. A delicious, spicy winter dish made originally from the delicate passenger pigeon or tourtes, it is comforting and rich. Today, with passenger pigeons extinct, different mixtures of meat are used. No need to wait for Christmas, enjoy tourtière hot or cold.

1 9-inch/23cm unbaked double	½ tsp ground cloves
pastry shell	1 tsp thyme
1½ lb/750g lean minced pork	½ tsp mustard
1 lb/500g minced beef	½ pt/4 fl oz/½ cup water
1 onion, minced	½ pt/4 fl oz/½ cup beef stock
1 clove garlic, minced	or red wine
1 tsp salt	3 potatoes, boiled and mashed
1 tsp pepper	1 egg, beaten
½ tsp cinnamon	

Pre-heat oven to gas mark 6, 400°F, 200C. Combine all ingredients, except the pastry, potatoes, and beaten egg, in a heavy saucepan and cook over low heat until the meat has changed colour. Cover and cook for about 45 minutes to 1 hour. Stir in the mashed potatoes and allow to cool. Fill the pastry shell with the meat mixture and cover with the other crust. Prick the pastry, glaze with a beaten egg, and bake for 40–45 minutes.

Green Tomato Ketchup

8lbs/3 kg/16 cups sliced green tomatoes	2pts/1¼ ltrs/4 cups white vinegar
4lbs/1½ kg/8 cups sliced onion	3 cups brown sugar
6oz/175g/³⁄₄ cup salt	4oz/125g/½ cup pickling spice, tied in a muslin bag

(makes 2 pints)

Layer the tomato and onion slices in a large dish, sprinkling each layer with salt. Cover with water and leave at room temperature for 24 hours. Drain and place in a saucepan. Add the vinegar, brown sugar and pickling spice, bring the mixture to the boil and simmer for 20 minutes. Stir well. Pour immediately into sterilized jars and seal.

Cash's Special Thanksgiving Turkey

Time for a hoe-down! Seasonal festivals have always been celebrated in Canada, whether it's a "sugaring-off" party, "apple-paring" bee, "barn-raising", or "strawberry festival". In Canada, Thanksgiving is held on the second Monday in October when families sit down to a harvest feast of roast turkey, sweet potatoes, corn, squash, garden vegetables, pickles and cranberry relish, all topped off with pumpkin pie and whipped cream. This unusual turkey recipe is well worth all the basting work – it finally emerges with a black caramelised skin, meat so tender it falls off the bone and a flavour that is out of this world!

Stuffing

1 tbsp butter	1 10oz/283g/1½ cups cranberries
8oz/225g/1 cup finely chopped onion	8oz/225g/2 cups breadcrumbs
	2 large bunches parsley, cleaned and chopped
8oz/225g/1 cup chopped mushrooms	1 tsp paprika
8oz/225g/1 cup chopped walnuts	2 tsp oregano
	salt and pepper
8oz/225g/1 cup chopped celery	1 beaten egg
8oz/225g/1 cup finely diced spicy sausage	

Melt the butter in a frying pan and lightly fry the onions, mushrooms, walnuts, celery, sausage and cranberries. Stir in the breadcrumbs and the remaining ingredients and set aside.

The Bird:

1 8–10 lb/3.6kg—4.5kg turkey	1 pt/600ml/2 cups water
	1 lemon, sliced
	2 vegetable stock cubes
½ bottle cognac	2 bay leaves
1 bottle Madeira or sherry	1 tsp fresh nutmeg
2 tbsp melted butter	1 tbsp basil

Stuff the turkey cavity loosely. Bake any left-over stuffing in a separate dish. Place turkey in a deep roasting pan and arrange the lemon slices between the wings, thighs and drumsticks. Pour the cognac, Madeira and melted butter over the turkey and add the water to the liquid in the bottom of the pan. (This ensures there'll be no flames!) Add the stock cubes and bay leaves and sprinkle with

28

the nutmeg and basil. Roast the turkey in a gas mark 8, 450°F, 230°C oven, basting every 20 minutes. Cover with aluminium foil after the first hour of cooking. Allow 20 minutes per pound plus an extra 20 minutes.

Barbecued Alberta Prime Beef Steak

The barbecue is the warm heart of western hospitality. Even in 40° below temperatures the barbecue will be glowing on the patio, the host huddled in his fur-lined parka and stetson, carefully grilling steaks for twelve.

4 x 1–1½ in/1 cm thick prime rib steaks (about 8oz/225g each)
black pepper

Have the barbecue coals hot and glowing. Season the steaks with freshly ground black pepper and put straight onto the rack about 6–8 inches from the fire. Flip after 3 minutes for rare. (Cook 3 minutes each side for rare. For well done, cook 7 minutes first side, 4 minutes second side.) Serve immediately with baked potatoes that have been wrapped in foil and cooked in the ashes, about 30–40 minutes, or until you can smell them.

Indian Style Cedar-Baked Salmon Fillets with Kelp

Long before the coming of the Europeans, the smell of burning alder wood permeated Canadian forests and shores as native peoples smoked their salmon draped on poles in cedar tents. They would let the fish cure for at least six days, and the salmon "jerky" would keep them in food for the winter. Another way of preserving the salmon was to "plank" it by splitting and nailing the fish, skin side down, to a cedar slab and propping it near an open fire to cook slowly.

2 lb/1kg salmon fillet
2 fl oz/3 tbsp/¼ cup olive oil
juice and grated zest of 1 lemon or orange
½ tsp salt
1 tsp freshly ground black pepper

Marinate the salmon in the remaining ingredients for at least 1 hour. Meanwhile, soak a piece of cedar plank (untreated) in cold water for an hour and bake it for 5–10 minutes in a gas mark 8, 450°F, 230°C oven. Remove the salmon from the marinade, lay it on the plank and bake in the hot oven, allowing about 8 minutes per finger thickness of fish. Serve with kelp on the side.

Kelp

Bull kelp, a rich source of iron and protein, grows abundantly in the waters off the west coast of Vancouver Island, where it was dried and eaten as a vegetable by the native peoples. A part of the heritage of Japanese-Canadians, seaweeds are making a comeback in Canada as a health food.

4oz/100g dried bull kelp	1 tbsp sesame oil
1 tbsp olive oil	juice of ½ lemon
1 tbsp sesame seeds	

Cut the kelp into large strips and stir-fry in the olive oil for 1–2 minutes. Add the sesame seeds and cook until lightly browned. Just before serving stir in the sesame oil and lemon juice.

Barbecued Whole Salmon with Rhubarb and Wild Rice Stuffing

Oh, the lure of the wild! Wild salmon, wild rhubarb, wild rice! Pick any salmon from the Pacific Ocean varieties of sockeye, spring, chinook, chum and coho, or choose Atlantic salmon. A typical Canadian backyard will yield clumps of rhubarb, the ubiquitous "lemon of the north", but don't use the poisonous leaves. Splash out on some wild rice from the wetland areas of Manitoba and Ontario – well worth the extra dollars for this luxury grain – and impress your special guests with the natural taste of Canada.

8oz/250g/1 cup wild rice	1 egg, beaten
2 tbsp butter	1 tbsp brown sugar
8oz/250g/1 cup chopped rhubarb	½ tsp sage
	salt and pepper
3 green onions, finely chopped	1 whole 2–3 lb salmon, cleaned
1 stalk celery, finely chopped	

Stir the rice into 2½ pts/1½ ltr/5 cups of boiling water and boil for 5 minutes. Remove from the heat, cover and allow to sit for 1 hour.

Drain. Melt the butter in a saucepan and sauté the rhubarb, onion and celery until softened. Stir in the wild rice, egg, sugar, sage, salt and pepper and mix well. Stuff the salmon with this mixture, skewer and lace closed. Place on an oiled piece of foil and wrap loosely. Barbecue over medium heat for 10–12 minutes per inch thickness of fish plus an extra 10 minutes or bake in a gas mark 7, 450°F, 220°C oven, allowing the same amount of time. Bake any leftover stuffing separately.

Maritime Salt Cod and Potato Galettes with Applesauce

This is a variation on Hugger-in-Buff or Fish and Scrunchions of Newfoundland and the Maritimes, where salt cod was the mainstay of the Atlantic fisherman's diet. Here it is teamed with Prince Edward Island potatoes and given a hint of sweetness by Annapolis Valley apples. Perhaps you can still hear, whispering on the sea breeze, the old sailors clinking their tankards of Newfoundland Screech Rum and toasting, "Long may your big jib draw!"

1/2 lb/250g salt cod	2 eggs
2 rashers/1/4 cup diced Canadian back bacon	1 tbsp flour
	1/2 tsp baking powder
1 lb/500g/2 cups raw, grated potatoes	2 tbsp chopped parsley
	pinch salt
8oz/500g/1 cup raw, grated parsnips	1 tsp pepper
	1/2 tsp grated nutmeg
1/2 onion, grated	2 tbsp olive oil
1 tsp fresh grated ginger	

(makes 3–4)

Soak the cod in cold water for 24–48 hours, changing the water 2 or 3 times. Drain. Put into a saucepan, cover with water and simmer for about 15 minutes. Drain and flake. Fry the bacon in a frying pan until crisp, drain, then remove to a large mixing bowl. Add the cod and all the remaining ingredients, except olive oil, and mix well. Heat the oil in the frying pan and drop in 1–2 tablespoons of the mixture, flatten and fry until lightly browned on both sides (about 6–7 minutes). Keep warm and serve with applesauce.

Fresh Lake Trout in Corn Husks

Manitoba – "Land of 10,000 Lakes" – is home to Canada's famed goldeye, a freshwater fish named for the golden colour it acquires after being smoked. More readily obtainable but no less delicious is fresh rainbow trout. "Clean trout, rub well with salt, wrap in clean leaves, cover with mud and bury in hot ashes," suggests an anonymous angler, whose advice by all means try! Another recommends salting the skin of the trout, leaving for 20 minutes and broiling, whereupon the skin will take on rainbow colours. This method of wrapping in husks or leaves keeps the fish deliciously moist.

4 x ½ lb/250g rainbow trout, cleaned
2 tsp salt
2 tsp pepper
2 tbsp butter
1 lemon, sliced
grated zest of 1 lemon
4 ears of corn on the cob or 8 large romaine lettuce leaves

39

Pat each fish dry and rub inside and out with salt and pepper. Place a knob of butter and ¼ of the lemon zest inside each one and a slice of lemon on top. Soak the ears of corn in cold water for 15 minutes. Remove the cob and the silk from the ears and wrap a trout in each husk, tying at the open end. If using lettuce leaves, place each trout on a leaf, place another leaf on top and tie with string, making sure the lettuce is wrapped tightly around the fish. Either barbecue over medium heat for 15 minutes, turning once, or bake in a pre-heated gas mark 5, 375°F, 190°C oven for 10–15 minutes.

Boiled Atlantic Lobster with Drawn Butter and Lemon

Glistening blue lobsters straight from the Atlantic Ocean turn reddish-pink after boiling in sea water. If you're squeamish, try to avoid eye contact and use tongs and rubber gloves! Lobsters are wonderful and decadent and messy so forget being genteel, tuck your bib in, grasp your nutcrackers and hammers and dig in! What a treat – you need nothing more to complement lobster except a smooth buttery sauce, a crisp Canadian sparkling wine such as Summerhill Cipes Brut, and perhaps a simple wild berry tart to finish.

2 x 1–1½ lb/500–750g live lobsters

Keep the lobsters in a bag in the fridge until needed. Do not put them in fresh water or they will die. Fill a large saucepan with salted water, enough to cover the lobsters. Bring to the boil and plunge in the live lobsters. Bring back to the boil and cook the lobsters

at 10 minutes for 500g/1 lb, 10–12 minutes for 700g/1¼ lb and 12–15 minutes for 750g/1½ lb (approximately 10 minutes per 500g/pound). When they're cooked, plunge quickly into cold water to stop the cooking. Place on a board and split lengthwise with a sharp knife. Take out the stomach, the small sac under the eyes, and the dark vein that runs through the centre of the body. Do not discard the green liver or the red roe as they can be eaten. Arrange the lobster halves on a platter of watercress and serve with drawn butter and lemon wedges.

Drawn Butter

2 tbsp butter	½ tsp pepper
1 tbsp flour	½ pt/360ml/1 cup boiling water
pinch salt	1 tbsp lemon juice

Melt 1 tablespoon butter in a saucepan over low heat and blend in the flour, salt and pepper to make a roux. Gradually pour in the water, stirring all the time until thickened. Remove from the heat and whisk in the rest of the butter, piece by piece, and stir in the lemon juice.

Baked Squash

It's always a joy to see the sunny summer yellows and greens of courgettes and pattypan squash or the fall greens, golds and ambers of acorn, butternut, hubbard and turban squashes and pumpkin. Tumbling pyramids of these colourful vegetables brighten any urban and country market across Canada.

43

2 acorn or butternut squash   1 tsp pepper
2 tbsp butter   2¹/₂oz/75g/¹/₃ cup
2 tbsp maple syrup   chopped pecans
pinch salt

Cut the squash in half, remove the seeds and place, cut side down, in a greased baking dish. Bake in a gas mark 5, 375°F, 190°C oven for about 50 minutes or until tender. Remove, scoop out the flesh and mix with the rest of the ingredients. Fill each half with the mixture, drizzle with more maple syrup and butter and return to the oven. Bake until the top is glazed and serve hot.

Boiled and Barbecued Corn from Bear Paw

Influenced by the native peoples, early settlers planted corn as one of their first crops. Eaten fresh from the cob, cooked with beans in a succotash, or dried and ground into "Indian meal" and baked into corn breads or johnny cakes, corn was a vital part of the homesteader's diet. A friend from Bear Paw in the foothills of the Rocky Mountains recalls late-summer corn boil parties of the 1950s that were well fueled with strong Canadian beer.

To Boil: Remove the husks and silk from four ears of corn. Bring a large saucepan of water to the boil and plunge in the corn. Cook for 4–6 minutes for young corn and 10 minutes for older corn. Serve with butter, salt and pepper.

To Barbecue: Soak four ears of corn, including the husks, in cold water for 30 minutes. Place on the barbecue grill and cook for 15–20 minutes over high heat. Remove from heat, pull back the husks, discarding the silk, to form a handle and eat with butter, salt and pepper.

44

Wildflower Salad and Raspberry Vinaigrette

Flowers and herbs feature profusely in grandmother's recipe and home remedy books. In her day she didn't have to worry about chemicals and pesticides, but today it is important that the flowers used are organically grown. The sturdy fireweed is the flower symbol of the Yukon and can be eaten raw or cooked as greens. So-called Fiddleheads are the edible fronds of the ostrich fern. Because of their resemblance to the scrolled top of a violin, these springtime delicacies are native to New Brunswick (but can be bought frozen now). Their taste is slightly similar to asparagus.

½ lb/250g/2 cups young dandelion leaves, washed and torn
½ lb/250g/2 cups young beet leaves, washed and torn
½ lb/250g/2 cups fireweed, washed and torn,
    or young spinach leaves
½ lb/250g/2 cups watercress, washed
4oz/125g/1 cup arugula, washed and torn
1 small red leaf lettuce, washed and torn
½ lb/250g/2 cups fiddleheads, washed and lightly scraped,
    or 1 bunch asparagus, chopped
edible flowers such as borage, calendula, nasturtium,
    pansies, roses, violets, day lilies and chive flowers

Dressing:
2 tbsp raspberry vinegar
2 tbsp lemon juice
2 fl oz/3tbsp/¼ cup walnut oil
2 fl oz/3tbsp/¼ cup olive oil
salt and pepper
½ tsp sugar

Quickly cook the fiddleheads (or asparagus) in boiling, salted water for 3–5 minutes. Plunge into cold water and drain well. Mix with the rest of the ingredients and toss with the raspberry vinaigrette dressing.

Quebec Sugar Pie

Lac des Sables, north of Montreal, conjures up memories of crisp fall mornings, vivid red and gold maple trees, *pain dorés* (French toast), hot chocolate and sugar pie. Wonderfully creamy and sweet, sugar pie is made in many regions of Canada. In Quebec *les habitants* learned the indigenous method of tapping maple trees for sap and would have used maple syrup or maple sugar for their pies instead of brown sugar.

1 9-in/23cm single unbaked pastry shell
1¼lb/600g/2 cups brown sugar
4oz/125g/½ cup chopped walnuts
2 tbsp butter
few drops vanilla
¾pt/420ml/1½ cups whipping cream

Spread the sugar over the unbaked pastry case. Sprinkle with walnuts and dot with butter. Mix the vanilla with the cream and pour over the sugar. Place in a pre-heated gas mark 5, 375°F, 190°C oven for 30–35 minutes. Serve warm or cold.

Nanaimo Bars

It's a mystery how this delightful confection came to be associated with the old coal mining town of Nanaimo on the east coast of Vancouver Island. Captain Vancouver arrived in these waters in 1792 when the region was the home of five native tribes. His log has no mention of Nanaimo Bars so at least we can narrow the time of their invention to the last two hundred years. What is certain is that everyone who tries one loves it!

4oz/125g/½ cup butter	**Topping:**
2oz/50g/¼ cup sugar	3 tbsp milk
5 tbsp cocoa	2 tbsp custard powder
1 tsp vanilla	2oz/50g/¼ cup butter
1 egg	1lb/500g/2 cups icing sugar,
½lb/250g/2 cups digestive	sifted
biscuit crumbs	4oz/squares semi-sweet
4oz/125g/½ cup chopped	chocolate
walnuts	1 tbsp butter

In a bowl, soften the butter and mix with the sugar, cocoa, vanilla and egg. Set in boiling water and stir until the butter has melted and the mixture resembles thick custard. Mix in the crumbs and nuts and pack into a 9-in/23 cm square tin.

For the topping, mix the milk and custard powder together and cream with the butter. Blend in the icing sugar and spread over the chocolate crumb base. Allow to stand for 15 minutes to harden slightly. Melt the chocolate and butter in a bowl over hot water and drizzle over the top of the custard. Allow to stand until set, then cut into squares and watch them disappear!

Wilderness Energy Bars

Fruit "trail mixes" and "energy bars" are the modern over-the-counter descendants of the pioneers' "jerky" and "pemmican". Dried and pounded fruits and meats were the natural answer to problems of travelling and winter storage. Pemmican is cooked and pounded buffalo meat mixed with hot grease and dried chokecherries or berries. Stored in bags made of animal hide and buried, it kept for years if necessary. This more modern version won't stay long in your backpack as you munch your way through cedar forest trails and along ocean bluffs or mountain paths.

4oz/125g/¹/₂ cup butter
6oz/175g/³/₄ cup brown sugar
¹/₄pt/5 fl oz/¹/₂ cup honey
2 tbsp peanut butter
10oz/300g/2¹/₂ cups raisin bran
1lb/500g/2 cups rolled oats
8oz/250g/1 cup granola
4oz/125g/¹/₂ cup chopped dried
  apricots

4oz/125g/¹/₂ cup grated coconut,
  unsweetened
4oz/125g/¹/₂ cup sunflower seeds
4oz/125g/¹/₂ cup chopped
  almonds
4oz/125g/¹/₄ cup sesame seeds

(makes 27)

Melt the butter in a large pan and stir in the sugar, honey and peanut butter. Stir until smooth and syrupy. Add all the remaining ingredients and stir well. Cook for about 5–10 minutes or until everything starts turning golden brown. Spoon into a greased 13 in/23 cm square baking tin. Press down and leave to cool. Slice into bars. These are very rich and they freeze well.

Lac St. Jean Hot Blueberry Cake

Blueberries are native to many regions of Canada, including Lac St. Jean in northern Quebec which is reputed to have the finest. Blueberries can be eaten fresh off the bush, mixed with wild strawberries and swimming in cream, or made into this rich, moist cake topped with a cinnamon crumble and bursting with delicious blue explosions. Serve with fresh cream or ice-cream.

Crumble:
2¹/₂oz/75g/¹/₃ cup brown sugar
2oz/50g/¹/₄ cup flour
¹/₂ tsp cinnamon
1 tbsp butter, melted

Cake:
8oz/250g/1 cup flour
2 tsp baking powder

2¹/₂oz/75g/¹/₃ cup sugar
¹/₂ tsp salt
¹/₄pt/10 fl oz/¹/₂ cup milk
2 tbsp butter, melted
1 egg
¹/₂lb/250g/1 cup blueberries
(fresh or frozen)

In a bowl, mix the brown sugar, flour, cinnamon and butter together and set aside. In a separate bowl, sift together the flour, baking powder, sugar and salt. Beat the milk, butter and egg together and stir into the flour until lightly mixed. Pour into a greased 9 inch/23 cm square cake tin. Sprinkle the blueberries over the batter and top with the crumble mix. Bake in a pre-heated gas mark 5, 375°F, 190°C oven for 45–55 minutes.

Butter Tarts

These golden delights are unique to Canada but no one is sure of their origin. Butter tarts may be an adaptation of Louisiana's pecan pie, or a variation on Quebec's sugar pie – perhaps someone mistakenly left out the flour from raisin pies and, afraid to lose face, called the rich, buttery, feather-light concoctions "butter tarts"!

2oz/50g/¹/₄ cup butter
4oz/125g/¹/₂ cup brown sugar
¹/₂ tsp vanilla
1 egg
2 fl oz/3tbsp/¹/₄ cup dark corn syrup
4oz/125g/¹/₂ cup raisins
1 tbsp lemon juice
12 unbaked tart shells

Cream the butter, sugar and vanilla. Beat in the egg and syrup. Stir in the raisins and lemon juice. Pour into the tart shells and bake in a pre-heated gas mark 5, 375°F, 190°C oven for 15–20 minutes.

Drinks

In the early days, home-made brews or "white lightning" were to be found throughout Canada. There was Caribou from a mixture of white wine and gin (dandelion wine would have been used); Newfoundland "Swish", a homemade rum; spruce beer from spruce boughs, molasses and yeast; Yukon "hootch" from sourdough and sugar; and a variety of beers and ciders.

Bloody Caesar or Howdy

This is a modern classic Canadian drink similar to a Bloody Mary but using a mixture of clam juice and tomato juice called "clamato". If you can't find clamato juice mix $^2/_3$ tomato juice, with $^1/_3$ clam juice.

1 lime	4oz/100ml clamato juice
salt or celery salt	2–3 drops Tabasco
ice cubes	2–3 drops Worcestershire sauce
2oz/50ml vodka	1 stalk celery

Rub the rim of a glass with a lime wedge and dip into a saucer of either salt or celery salt. Add ice cubes. Pour in the vodka, clamato juice, Tabasco and Worcestershire sauce and stir. Serve with a squeeze of lime, a lime wedge and a celery stalk.

Canadian Manhattan

Canadian rye whisky has a reputation as widely known as that of the grain from which it is distilled. Of the many cocktails that find their source on the Canadian prairie, this is a favourite.

2oz/50ml Canadian Club rye whisky
1oz/25ml sweet Vermouth
2–3 drops Angostura bitters
ice cubes

Stir the rye, vermouth, bitters and ice together and strain into a cocktail glass. Serve with a cherry or lemon twist.

Have a nice day, eh!

Index